THE WORLD OF OCEAN ANIMALS
SPONGES

by Mari Schuh

pogo

Ideas for Parents and Teachers

Pogo Books let children practice reading informational text while introducing them to nonfiction features such as headings, labels, sidebars, maps, and diagrams, as well as a table of contents, glossary, and index.

Carefully leveled text with a strong photo match offers early fluent readers the support they need to succeed.

Before Reading

- "Walk" through the book and point out the various nonfiction features. Ask the student what purpose each feature serves.
- Look at the glossary together. Read and discuss the words.

Read the Book

- Have the child read the book independently.
- Invite him or her to list questions that arise from reading.

After Reading

- Discuss the child's questions. Talk about how he or she might find answers to those questions.
- Prompt the child to think more. Ask: Sponges are animals that look like plants. How are sponges different from other animals?

Pogo Books are published by Jump!
5357 Penn Avenue South
Minneapolis, MN 55419
www.jumplibrary.com

Library of Congress Cataloging-in-Publication Data

Names: Schuh, Mari C., 1975- author.
Title: Sponges / by Mari Schuh.
Description: Minneapolis: Jump!, Inc., [2024]
Series: The world of ocean animals | Includes index.
Audience: Ages 7-10
Identifiers: LCCN 2023008480 (print)
LCCN 2023008481 (ebook)
ISBN 9798885245807 (hardcover)
ISBN 9798885245814 (paperback)
ISBN 9798885245821 (ebook)
Subjects: LCSH: Sponges–Juvenile literature.
Classification: LCC QL371.6 .S38 2024 (print)
LCC QL371.6 (ebook)
DDC 593.4–dc23/eng/20230323
LC record available at https://lccn.loc.gov/2023008480
LC ebook record available at https://lccn.loc.gov/2023008481

Editor: Jenna Gleisner
Designer: Molly Ballanger

Photo Credits: John A. Anderson/Shutterstock, cover, 10-11tl, 14-15; Francesco_Ricciardi/Shutterstock, 1; Richard Whitcombe/Shutterstock, 3, 20-21; Seadam/ Dreamstime, 4; BIOSPHOTO/Alamy, 5; Damsea/ Shutterstock, 6-7, 8-9; Henryp982/Shutterstock, 10-11tr; Alexey Masliy/Shutterstock, 10-11bl; imageBROKER/ Norbert Probst/SuperStock, 10-11br; Eric Carlander/ Shutterstock, 12; Jolanta Wojcicka/Shutterstock, 13; Ethan Daniels/Shutterstock, 16; Placebo365/iStock, 17; Fred Bavendam/Minden Pictures/SuperStock, 18-19; RLS Photo/Shutterstock, 23.

Printed in the United States of America at Corporate Graphics in North Mankato, Minnesota.

TABLE OF CONTENTS

CHAPTER 1

UNUSUAL ANIMALS

Colorful ocean life covers a **coral reef**. Sponges live on the reef. Some look like plants. But they are animals!

sponge ·····▶

There are more than 8,000 sponge **species**. They live in every ocean. They are found in both **shallow** and deep water.

Each sponge has a skeleton covered with tough skin. Some sponges are hard. Others are soft and **flexible**.

DID YOU KNOW?

Sponges do not have **organs**. This means they don't have body parts like hearts, stomachs, or eyes.

Sponges come in many colors, shapes, and sizes. Sponges that live in shallow water are usually bright. Sunlight helps give them their colors.

stove-pipe
sponge

giant barrel
sponge

orange encrusting
sponge

green finger
sponge

Some sponges look like tubes, vases, or fans. Others are flat. Some look like bushes or branches.

DID YOU KNOW?

Some sponges are as tiny as beans. Others can be more than six feet (1.8 meters) tall!

CHAPTER 2

LIFE UNDERWATER

Sponges attach to the seafloor or hard, rocky surfaces. They attach using a part called a holdfast. Most sponges stay in one place.

holdfast

Water flows into a sponge's **pores** and through its **chambers**. **Cells** inside **filter** the water. This is how sponges breathe and eat. The cells take **oxygen** and bits of food from the water.

pore

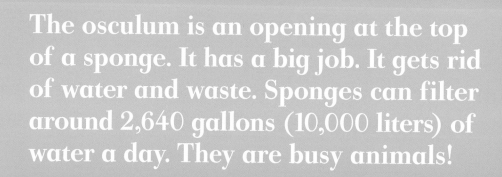

osculum

The osculum is an opening at the top of a sponge. It has a big job. It gets rid of water and waste. Sponges can filter around 2,640 gallons (10,000 liters) of water a day. They are busy animals!

TAKE A LOOK!

How does water move through a sponge? Take a look!

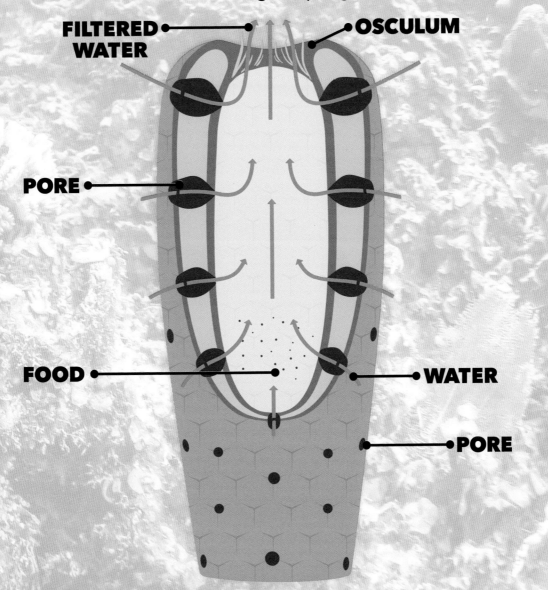

FILTERED WATER

OSCULUM

PORE

FOOD

WATER

PORE

CHAPTER 3

HELPING OUT

Sponges give other animals places to hide and rest. Many plants and animals make their homes on sponges. Worms and shrimp live inside some.

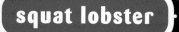

squat lobster

Sponges can be home to just a few animals. Or they might have hundreds! A sponge's many chambers are great spots for animals to hide.

eel ····▶

Sponges can also serve as **camouflage**. A sponge crab holds a piece of a sponge against its shell. This helps the crab blend in. It can hide from **predators** such as fish.

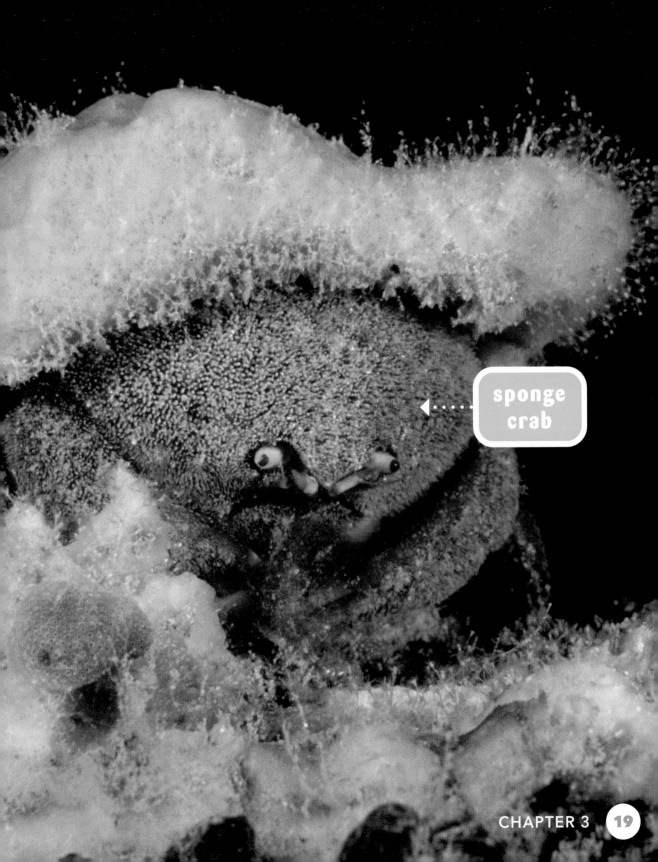

sponge crab

Parts of a sponge can break off. But that's OK. Why? The sponge can grow new parts! And that's not all. A whole new sponge can grow from one small piece. Sponges can grow again from just a few cells. No other animal can do that!

Sponges are unique animals. What more would you like to learn about them?

DID YOU KNOW?

Some sponges can sneeze! One sponge sneeze can last about 30 minutes. Sponges sneeze to get rid of **mucus**.

TRY THIS!

MAKE A WATER FILTER

Sponges filter water to get food and oxygen. Make your own water filter with this fun activity.

What You Need:

- plastic water bottle with cap
- scissors
- small pushpin
- two coffee filters
- two cotton balls
- spoon
- craft sand
- playground sand
- gravel
- muddy water

1. Ask an adult to cut the empty water bottle in half and use the pushpin to poke a few holes in the water bottle's cap.

2. Place two coffee filters in the top half of the water bottle.

3. Tear the cotton balls into pieces. Set them inside the coffee filters.

4. Measure two spoonfuls of the craft sand. Pour them into the coffee filters. Do the same with the playground sand. Add the gravel last so they are layered.

5. Place the top half of the water bottle into the bottom half with the cap facing down.

6. Now pour the muddy water into the coffee filter. Water should drip into the bottom half of the water bottle. What does the water look like? How did the sand and gravel help filter the muddy water?

camouflage: A disguise or natural coloring that allows animals to hide by making them look like their surroundings.

cells: The smallest parts of an animal or plant.

chambers: Enclosed spaces.

coral reef: A long line of coral that lies in warm, shallow water.

filter: To take in water, separate and keep the parts of it that are wanted, and get rid of the rest.

flexible: Able to bend or move easily.

mucus: A thick, slimy liquid.

organs: Parts of the body that have certain purposes.

oxygen: A colorless gas found in air and water. Humans and animals need oxygen to breathe.

pores: Tiny holes.

predators: Animals that hunt other animals for food.

shallow: Not deep.

species: One of the groups into which similar animals and plants are divided.

INDEX

TO LEARN MORE

Finding more information is as easy as 1, 2, 3.

1. **Go to www.factsurfer.com**
2. **Enter "sponges" into the search box.**
3. **Choose your book to see a list of websites.**

FACT SURFER